My Perfectly Pretty Book

Illustrated by Nellie Ryan,
Katy Jackson, Hannah Davies
and Beth Gunnell

Edited by Bryony Jones

Designed by John Bigwood
Cover design by Angie Allison

W www.busterbooks.co.uk
f Buster Children's Books
Y @BusterBooks

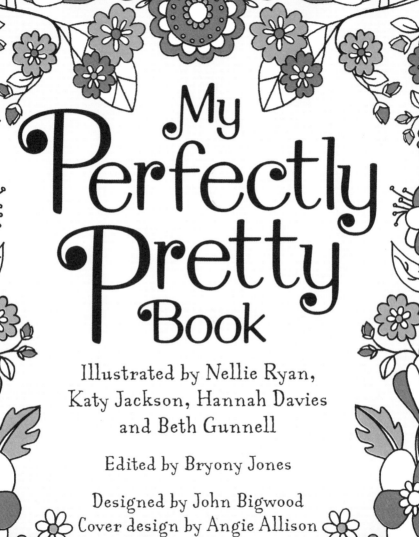

Buster Books

It's time to create
something beautiful.

Doodle, draw and colour your way through
this book, creating your own masterpieces.
You can use felt-tip pens, pencils or crayons
to design your works of art.

If you are drawing on top of coloured areas
on the page, leave your ink to dry for a
moment to avoid smudges.

The pictures in this
book were created,
coloured and completed by
Erin Brown ☺
....

Fill the page with flowers
and hummingbirds.

Fill the bathroom with lotions, potions and bubbles.

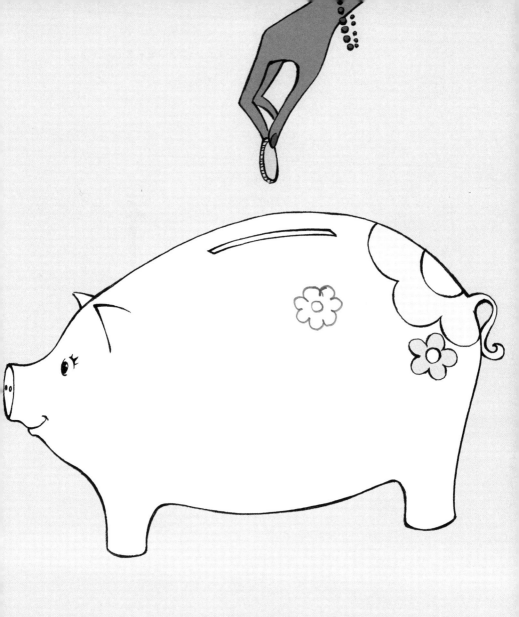

Decorate this sweet piggy bank.

Colour in this gorgeous garden pattern.

How does her garden grow? Fill it with plants and flowers.

Finish her patchwork quilt.

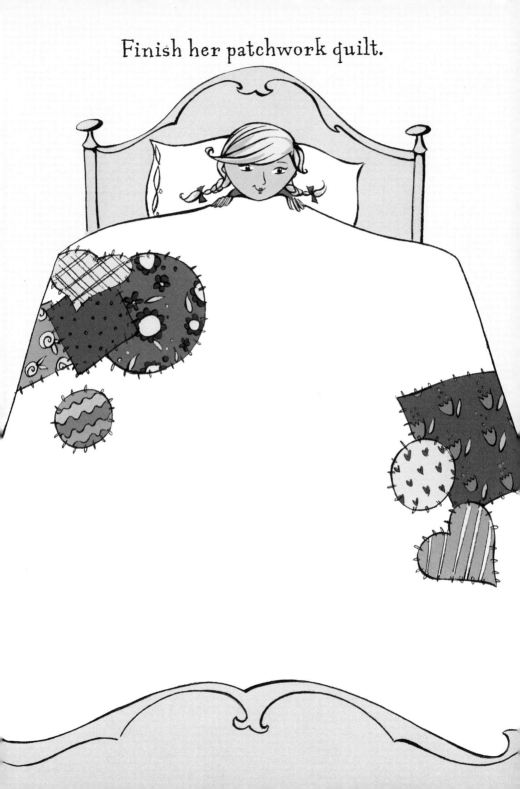

Decorate the beautiful bunting.

What's jumping through the hoop?

Boxes come in all shapes and sizes.
Decorate this stack.

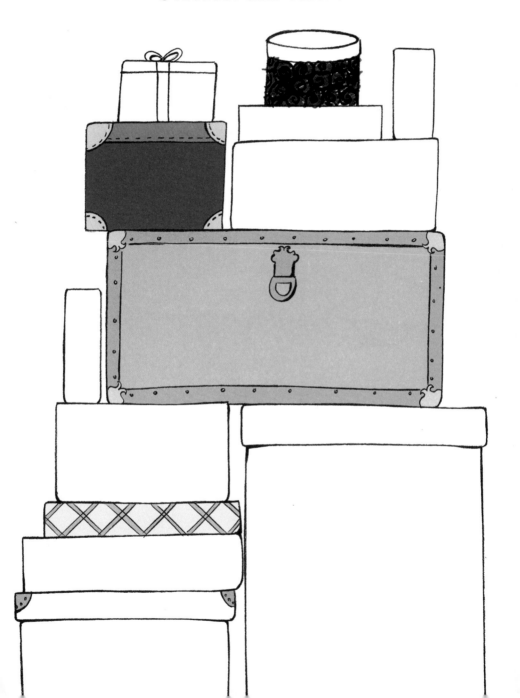

Colour this
nautical
design.

Fill her boudoir with beautiful things.

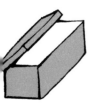

Fill the flask with a love potion.

Finish his tail with fabulous feathers.

Draw more mermaids at the party.

Customize her car.

Colour this
beautiful
bird pattern.

What's in the shop window?

What is she drawing in the sand?

Design some beautiful book covers and fill the shelves.

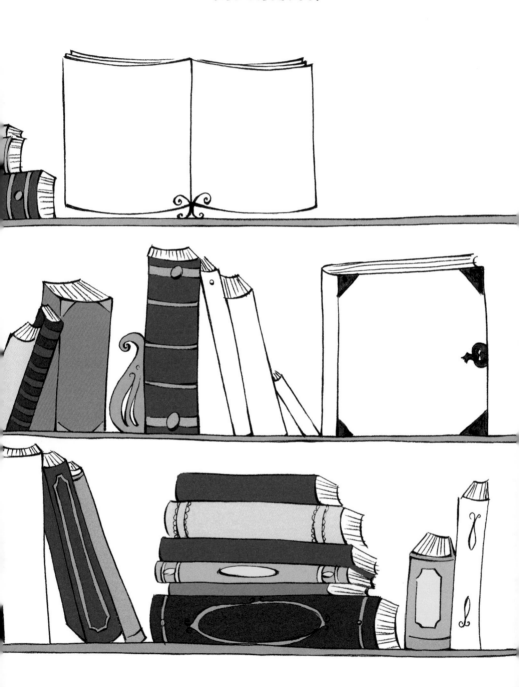

Add more cute chicks hatching from their shells.

Design your own sensational stationery.

Colour these tasty cupcakes.

Give the fairy a fabulous
pair of wings.

Furnish the doll's house.

Give these surfers stylish surfboards.

What's in the frames?

Fill the pond with goldfish.

Colour in this
tea-set pattern.

Fill the sky with fireworks.

What's she daydreaming about?

Fill the vases with flowers.

What can you see in the crystal ball?

Finish the flower pattern.

Add colour to this Hawaiian pattern.

Finish off these delightful dandelions and fill the page with more.

Doodle some fan-tastic designs.

Plant some sunflowers.

Grow a beautiful bonsai tree.

Decorate this tower of gift boxes.

Colour in these pretty teacups.

Add some fun fridge magnets.

Where has the magic carpet taken her?

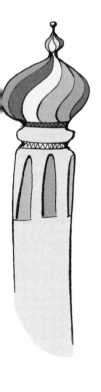

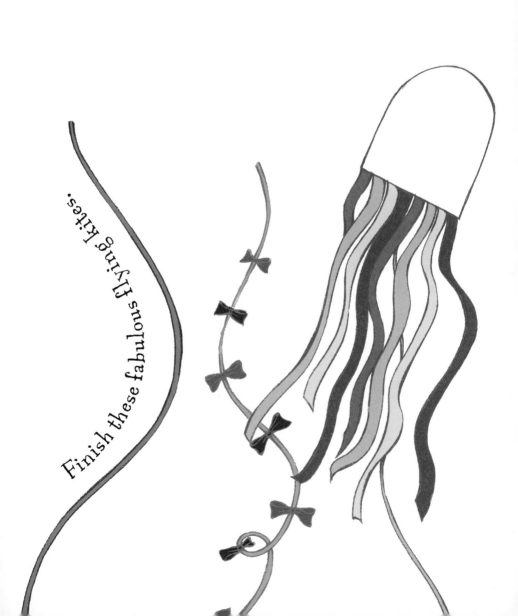

Finish these fabulous flying kites.

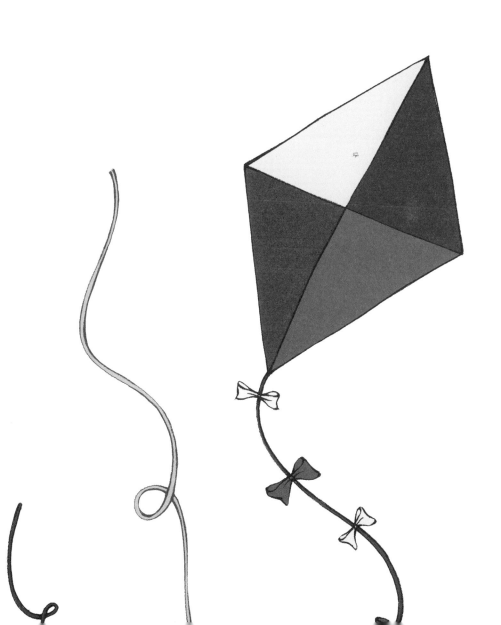

Pretty hearts
to colour.

Cover the sofa with bright and bold cushions.

Time for tea?

Design a pattern for the china here ...

... then decorate the tea set.

Decorate these trinket jars.

Ice the delicious biscuits.

What's your tile style? Add pictures and patterns to these tiles.

Colour in this
paisley pattern.

Design cute towels, swinging in the breeze.

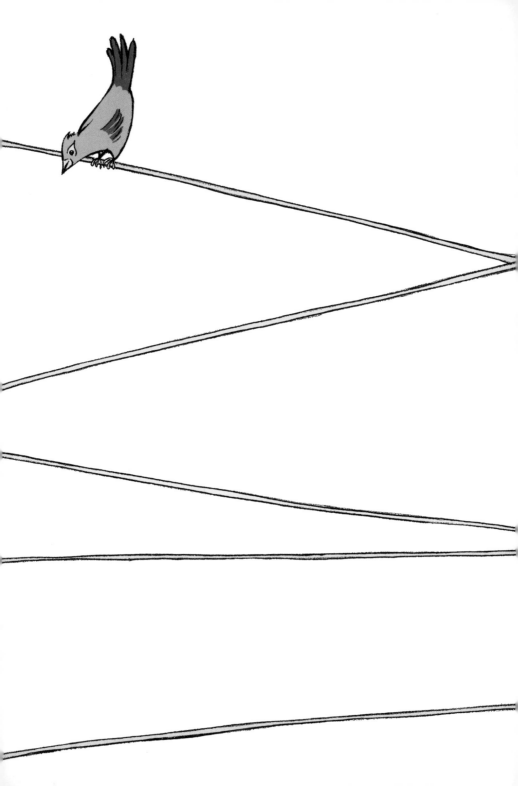

Draw more birds chilling out on the wires.

What's being sold in the
floating market?

Fill the page with tasty treats.

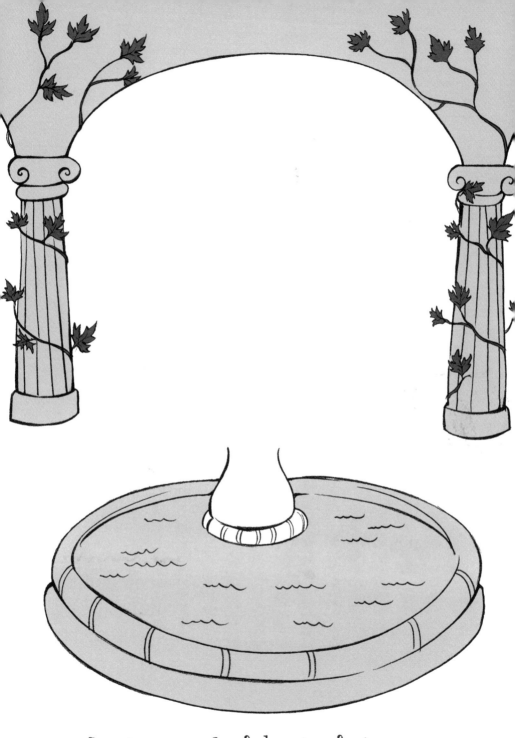

Create a wonderful water feature.

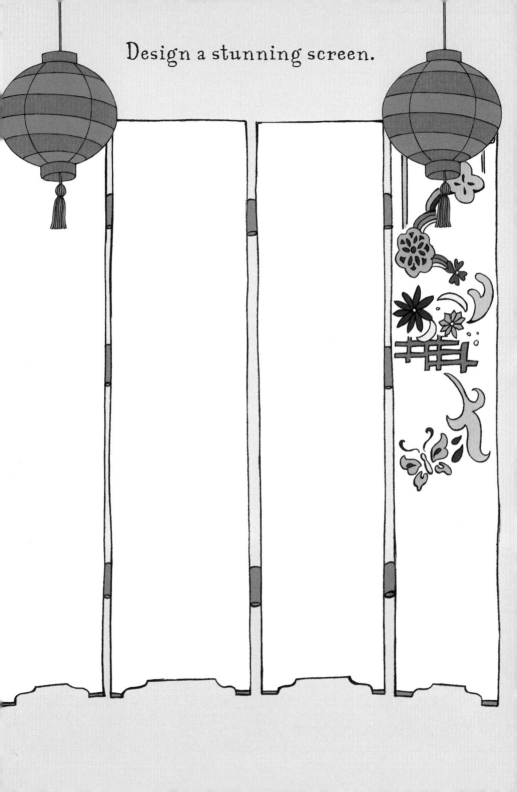

Design a stunning screen.

Fill the pots with bonkers bushes.

Decorate the tablecloth and hang more lanterns ...

... for the perfect outdoor banquet.

Colour these
brilliant butterflies.

Finish this marvellous mosaic.

Decorate these beautiful bowls.

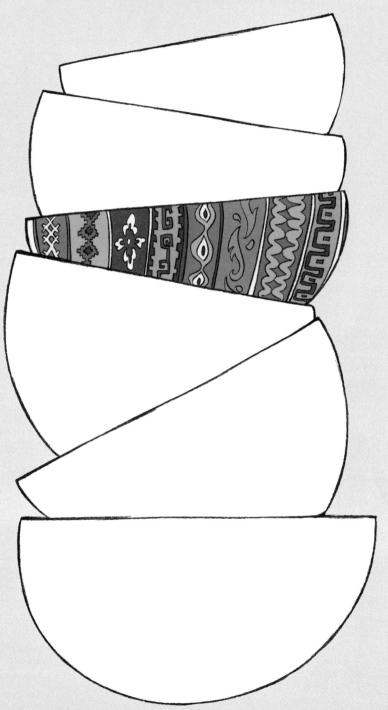

How will you fill the pick 'n' mix stand?

Give the castle towering turrets.

Colour this
terrific toadstool
pattern.

Time for a picnic. What are they eating?

Finish these Russian dolls.

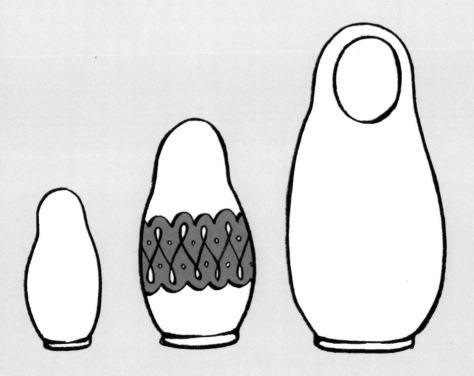

Colour in
this orchard
pattern.

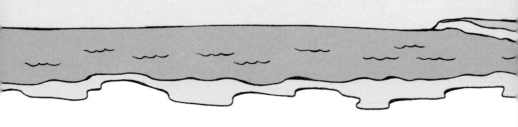

Add more seashells to the beach.

Yum! Draw your favourite ice cream.

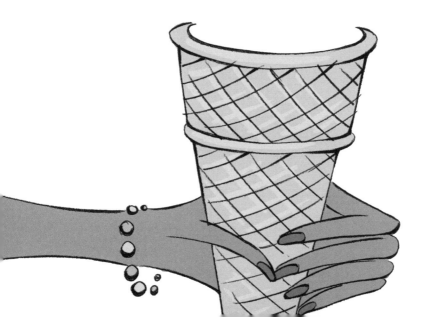

Design some cool album covers.

What can they pick from the tree?

Fill the frame.

Add more bubbles!

Colour in these zany flowers.

Add more cakes to the stand.

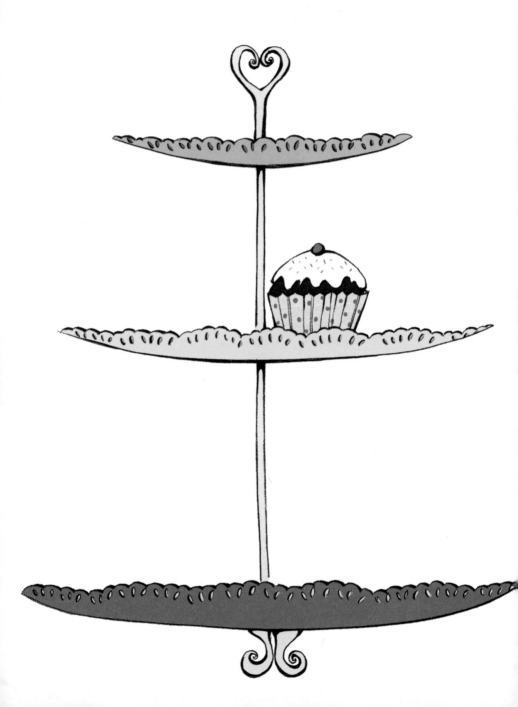

What's on the dressing table?

Where are these postcards from?

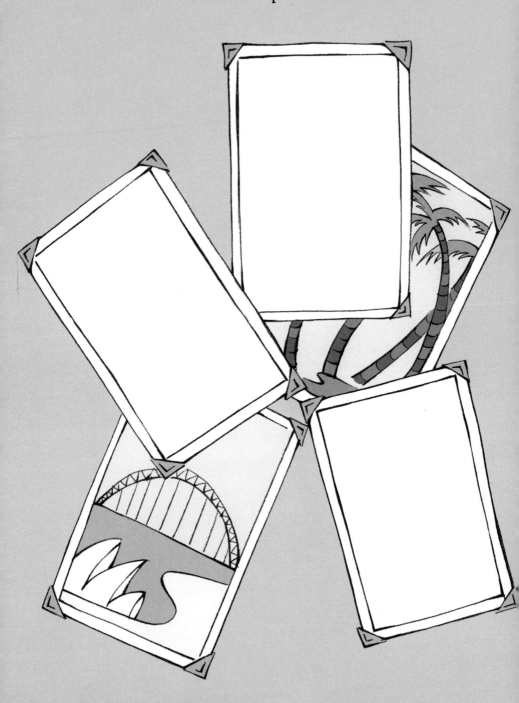

Allacazam! Draw what you have
wished for.

Colour these
totem poles.

What are they filming?

Draw what's in the attic.

Colour these
delightful domes.

What's in the party bag?

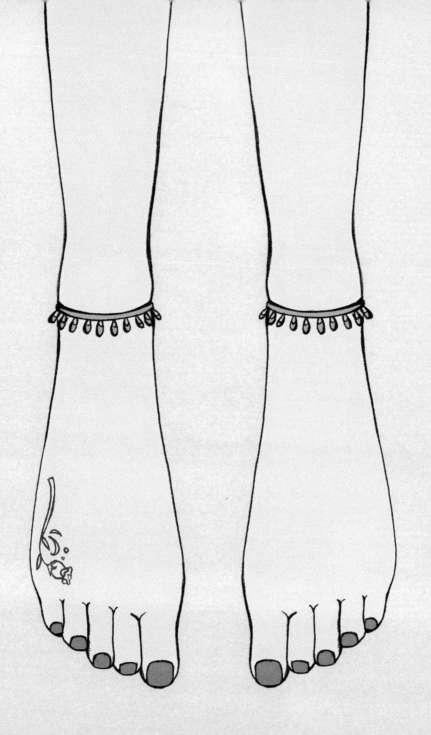

Paint her feet with henna.

Colour in this pretty plate.

First published in Great Britain in 2014 by Buster Books, an imprint of Michael O'Mara
Books Limited, 9 Lion Yard, Tremadoc Road, London SW4 7NQ.

The material in this book was adapted from ten titles previously published by Buster Books:
Beautiful Doodles, Beautiful Home Colouring Book, Fabulous Doodles, Girls' World, Holiday World,
Interior Designer Doodles, Patterns Around The World, Perfect Patterns,
Pretty Flower Patterns and *Pretty Patterns.*

ISBN: 978-1-78055-234-7

2 4 6 8 10 9 7 5 3

This book was printed in September 2015 by Leo Paper Products Ltd, Heshan Astros Printing
Limited, Xuantan Temple Industrial Zone, Gulao Town, Heshan City, Guangdong Province, China.